MONSTER B!RDS

ASHLEY GISH

T0002193

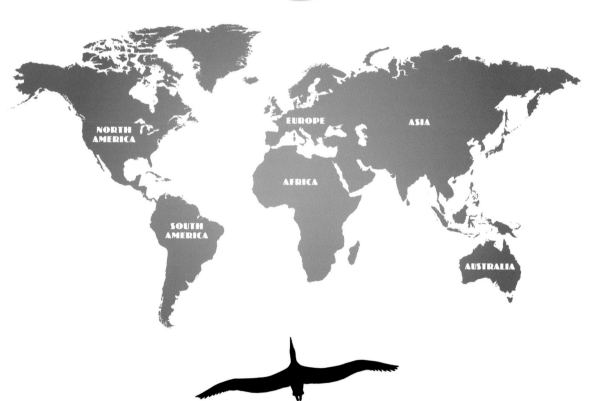

NORTH AMERICA

EUROPE

ASIA

AFRICA

SOUTH AMERICA

AUSTRALIA

CREATIVE EDUCATION · CREATIVE PAPERBACKS

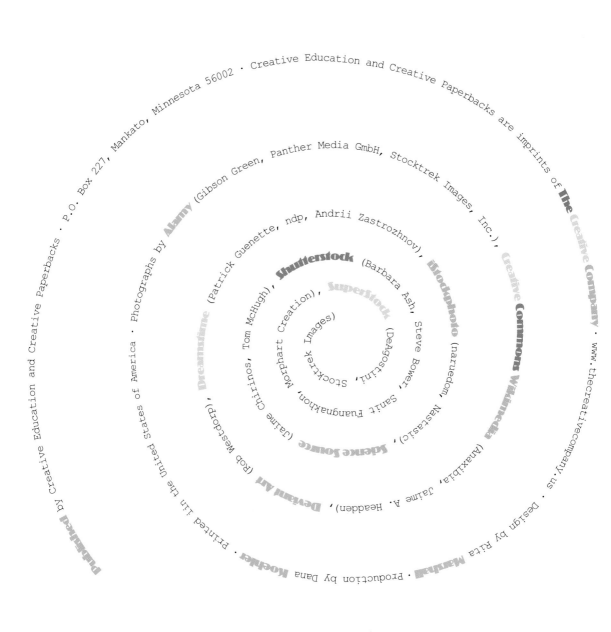

Published by Creative Education and Creative Paperbacks · P.O. Box 227, Mankato, Minnesota 56002 · Creative Education and Creative Paperbacks are imprints of The Creative Company · www.thecreativecompany.us · Design by Rita Marshall · Production by Dana Koehle · Printed in the United States of America · Photographs by Alamy (Gibson Green, Panther Media GmbH, Stocktrek Images, Inc.), Dreamstime (Patrick Guenette, ndp, Andrii Zastrozhnov), Shutterstock (Barbara Ash, Steve Bower, Sanit Fuangnakhon, Morphart Creation), Superstock (Stocktrek Images), iStockphoto (naruedom, Nastasic), Science Source (Jaime Chirinos, Tom McHugh), Deviant Art (Rob Westdorp), Jaime A. Headden)

Library of Congress Cataloging-in-Publication Data • Names: Gish, Ashley, author. • Title: Monster birds / by Ashley Gish. • Description: Mankato, Minnesota: The Creative Company, [2023] | Series: X-books: ice age creatures • Includes bibliographical references and index. • Audience: Ages 6–8 | Grades 2–3 | Summary: "A countdown of five of the most captivating monster bird fossil discoveries and relatives provides thrills as readers discover more about the biological, social, and hunting characteristics of these Ice Age creatures"—Provided by publisher. • Identifiers: LCCN 2021044446 | ISBN 9781640264366 (library binding) | ISBN 9781628329698 (paperback) | ISBN 9781640006102 (ebook) • Subjects: LCSH: Birds, Fossil—Juvenile literature. • Classification: LCC QE871 .G57 2023 | DDC 568—dc23/eng/20211116
LC record available at https://lccn.loc.gov/2021044446

MONSTER B!RDS

CONTENTS

ICE AGE CREATURES
BOOKS

Xceptional **ANCIENT ANIMALS** 5

Xciting **FACTS** 28

Xtreme **TOP 5 MONSTER BIRDS**

#5 **10**
#4 **16**
#3 **22**
#2 **26**
#1 **31**

Xasperating **CONFLICT** 25

Xemplary **DISCOVERIES** 20

Xtraordinary **LIFESTYLE** 18

GLOSSARY

RESOURCES

INDEX 32

XCEPTIONAL ANCIENT ANIMALS

Giant birds lived during the Ice Age. They thundered across the land. They soared overhead. They blotted out the sun. Monster birds ruled the land and sky.

Monster Bird Basics

Many kinds of monster birds lived during the Ice Age. Teratorns flew through the air. Terror birds walked on the land. Teratorns are related to modern vultures and eagles. Terror birds' closest living relatives are South America's seriemas.

MONSTER BIRDS

Monster birds lived throughout the continents of
North and South America.

▨ = monster bird fossil sites

NORTH
AMERICA

PANAMA

SOUTH
AMERICA

The Isthmus of Panama links North and South America.

LAND
BRIDGE

ARGENTAVIS MAGNIFICENS

23 feet (7 m) from

wing tip to wing tip

ANDEAN CONDOR

10.8 feet (3.3 m)

Some teratorns existed before the Ice Age. The giant teratorn weighed up to 159 pounds (72.1 kg). It lived about 9 to 7 million years ago. Its **fossils** have been found in Argentina. *Teratornis merriami* lived during the Ice Age. It weighed only 30 pounds (13.6 kg). Many of this bird's remains have been found in the La Brea Tar Pits in California.

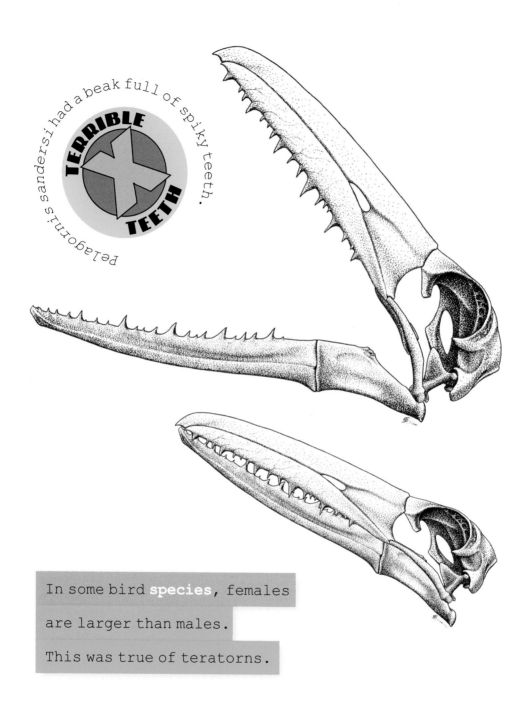

TERRIBLE TEETH

Pelagornis sandersi had a beak full of spiky teeth.

In some bird **species**, females are larger than males.

This was true of teratorns.

Terror birds had small wings. They could not fly. They ran quickly to catch prey. Most terror birds lived in South America. *Titanis walleri* was the only one in North America. It stood about five feet (1.5 m) tall. This giant died out early in the Ice Age.

Terror bird beaks were up to 18 inches (45.7 cm) long

BIG BEAKS

MONSTER BIRD BASICS FACT

Seriemas are medium-sized birds that live throughout

South America. Unlike terror birds, seriemas can fly.

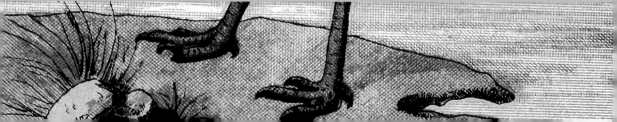

TOP FIVE XTREME MONSTER BIRDS

Xtreme Monster Bird #5

Ocean Glider Before the Ice Age, *Pelagornis sandersi* ruled the waters over eastern North America. It was the biggest flying bird ever. Its **wingspan** stretched more than 24 feet (7.3 m)! Modern seabirds need a running start to achieve flight. But this bird had small feet. It could not begin flight this way. Instead, it waited on the beach for a gust of wind to lift it into the air.

Monster Bird Beginnings

Earth was much cooler at the start of the Ice Age. Grasses and shrubs covered much of the land. Many animals thrived. Both plant- and meat-eaters found plenty of food. Animals, including some birds, grew large.

Aiolornis incredibilis means the "incredible bird god of the winds." This bird was the largest teratorn in North America. In 1993, part of a wing bone was discovered in Riverside County, California. It was well-preserved. This rare fossil helped scientists determine the bird's size. Its wingspan was more than 16 feet (4.9 m). It was the largest flying Ice Age bird.

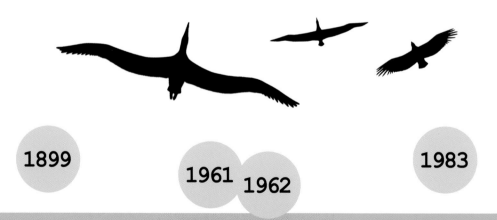

1899

Psilopterus fossil fragments, Argentina

1961 **1962**

Titanis walleri fossils, Florida

1983

Pelagornis sandersi fossil, South Carolina

1993

Aiolornis incredibilis
fossil, California

1999

Teratornis merriami
fossil, Oregon

At nearly 10 feet (3 m) tall, *Kelenken* may have been the tallest, fastest terror bird. It had the largest skull and strongest bite.

TOP FIVE XTREME MONSTER BIRDS

Xtreme Monster Bird #4

Small but Fierce *Psilopterus* (*sy-LOP-teh-rus*) were small terror birds. They stood about 30 inches (76.2 cm) tall but weighed up to 15 pounds (6.8 kg). Scientists think this bird leaped onto unsuspecting prey. Then it used its sharp claws to tear prey apart. Fossils in Uruguay suggest this bird may have lived as recently as 6,300 years ago. It resembled modern seriemas. They are small but fierce. Farmers keep seriemas to guard their chickens.

XTRAORDINARY LIFESTYLE

The La Brea Tar Pits and Anza-Borrego Desert State Park are both in California. These places are filled with the remains of **extinct** animals like teratorns. Fossils provide clues about how they lived.

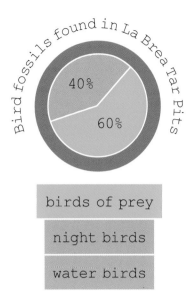

40%

60%

birds of prey

night birds

water birds

Monster Bird Society

Argentavis could fly. It had a wingspan of up to 23 feet (7 m). This huge monster bird could swallow hare-sized prey whole. But it likely preferred to tear food into pieces. Terror birds chased down small animals to eat. Scientists studied the leg bones of three terror bird species. The smallest was thought to be the fastest. It could likely run 60 miles (96.6 km) per hour.

Scientists in California have studied many teratorn fossils. Animals stuck in the tar pits attracted hungry monster birds. Then the teratorns became stuck there, too. Sixty percent of the bird fossils found at La Brea are from birds of prey. These include teratorns, eagles, and hawks.

South America's *Brontornis* stood more than nine feet

(2.7 m) tall. It is commonly called the thunder bird.

XEMPLARY DISCOVERIES

Bird bones have air holes inside them. This makes them lightweight. It helps birds fly. But these bones are fragile. They do not preserve well.

Scientists are excited when they discover bird fossils. Some *Aiolornis incredibilis* fossils have been discovered at Anza-Borrego Desert State Park. A life-sized model of this giant bird hangs in the park's visitor center.

Fossilized bones were found in the Santa Fe River near Gainesville, Florida, in the 1960s. Researchers believed the bones were from a horse. In the early 1990s, the bones were identified as belonging to a terror bird.

TOP FIVE XTREME MONSTER BIRDS

Xtreme Monster Bird #3

Fictional Monster Birds Giant birds have inspired writers and artists for years. J. R. R. Tolkien wrote about giant eagles in *The Hobbit* and *The Lord of the Rings*. They help Gandalf the wizard. Artists created props of the huge birds for movies based on the books. In 2013, two full-sized models of these eagles were put on display at the Wellington Airport in New Zealand. The eagles boasted wingspans of 45 feet (13.7 m)!

Monster birds lived in open grasslands and dry, wooded areas. The climate changed about 10,000 years ago. North America became wetter. Some birds could not adapt to these changes. Scientists use this information to predict how birds living today might adapt to climate change. If they cannot adapt, they could die off, too.

MONSTER BIRD SURVIVAL FACT

Today's monster birds include the wandering albatross, the Kori bustard, and the common ostrich.

XASPERATING CONFLICT

Scientists are not sure why monster birds died out. They do not think humans ever lived with these giant creatures. The changing climate likely hurt monster birds.

Monster Bird Survival

Some terror birds moved from South America to North America. At the same time, powerful predators such as saber-toothed cats and dire wolves spread into South America. There, they hunted the giant birds. Terror birds could not protect themselves against these powerful predators. Scientists think that many birds eventually went extinct because of **habitat** loss, though.

Xtreme Monster Bird #2

Condor Cousins Experts believe teratorns closely resembled modern condors. California and Andean condors are among the biggest flying birds alive today. Until recently, few California condors remained in the wild. Researchers caught the birds and bred them in captivity. Today, there are about 500 of these rare birds. Andean condors are also rare in the wild. But they are easy to spot when flying. Each one has about a 10-foot (3 m) wingspan!

Argentavis probably resembled modern condors, with a featherless head and neck and dark feathers elsewhere.

A bird's plumage includes all the feathers on its body. Brightly colored plumage attracts a mate. Duller colors help birds blend in with their surroundings.

Teratornis merriami lived throughout California, New Mexico, Florida, and parts of Mexico.

The only known *Pelagornis sandersi* fossil was found in South Carolina.

The common ostrich is the biggest, heaviest flightless bird today. It can be up to 8.5 feet (2.6 m) tall and nearly 300 pounds (136 kg)!

Toothed birds like *Pelagornis sandersi* mysteriously went extinct about 3 million years ago.

The name *Titanis* refers to the giant creatures from Greek mythology.

The wandering albatross has the widest wingspan today. It averages 10 feet (3 m). This seabird is a strong flier. It can cover up to 75,000 miles (120,701 km) per year!

Terror birds lived from 62 to 1.8 million years ago and mostly in South America

Humans never encountered terror birds. This was probably a good thing for humans!

Today, the Kori bustard is the heaviest flying bird. But it prefers to stay o the ground. When traveling in groups, these birds follow each other in a lir

One of the oldest terror birds is *Physornis*. Fossils have been found in southern Argentina dating to nearly 30 million years ago.

In 1909, the first extinct bird species from La Brea was described as originating from a teratorn.

Seriemas are aggressive hunters. They shake prey

violently in the air. Then they smash it to pieces against the ground before finally eating it.

TOP FIVE XTREME MONSTER BIRDS

Xtreme Monster Bird #1

Incredible Discovery The first *Aiolornis incredibilis* was found in Smith Creek Cave in Nevada in 1952. Out of nearly 650 bird bones, only a single bone from the wing of this teratorn was found. But it was enough for scientists to recognize a new species of monster bird. The bone was more than twice the size of similar *Teratornis merriami* bones. Later fossil finds led scientists to agree that *Aiolornis incredibilis* had a massive beak capable of shredding prey.

GLOSSARY

extinct – having no living members

fossils – the remains of once-living things preserved in rock

habitat – the natural home of plants and animals

species – a group of living beings that are closely related

wingspan – the longest measurement across the wings of an object or animal, from wing tip to wing tip

RESOURCES

"Our Birds." National Aviary. https://www.aviary.org/birds-habitats/our-birds.

Tite, Jack. *Mega Meltdown: The Weird and Wonderful Animals of the Ice Age*. New York: Blueprint Editions, 2018.

Riera, Lucas. *Extinct: An Illustrated Exploration of Animals That Have Disappeared*. New York: Phaidon Press, 2019.

INDEX

beaks 8, 9, 31

dangers 18, 19, 24, 25

extinction 8, 16, 18, 24, 25, 28

food 8, 12, 16, 19

hunting 8, 16, 19

other birds 5, 9, 10, 16, 19, 22, 25, 26, 28–29, 32

range 6, 8, 10, 12, 16, 18, 20, 21, 24, 25, 28

remains 7, 12, 16, 18, 19, 21, 28, 31

size 5, 7, 8, 10, 12, 15, 16, 19, 20, 31

wings 7, 8, 10, 12, 19, 31

Cassowaries are large, flightless birds. They live in Australia and on some neighboring islands. Deemed "the world's most dangerous bird," they are powerful enough to kill a human.